My First Time
Going to a Funeral

by Caryn Rivadeneira

LOOK!
BOOKS™

Red Chair Press   Egremont, Massachusetts

Look! Books are produced and published by Red Chair Press:

Red Chair Press LLC   PO Box 333   South Egremont, MA 01258-0333

FREE Educator Guides at www.redchairpress.com/free-resources

Publisher's Cataloging-In-Publication Data

Names: Rivadeneira, Caryn Dahlstrand, author.

Title: Going to a funeral / by Caryn Rivadeneira.

Description: Egremont, Massachusetts : Red Chair Press, [2021] | Series:
    Look! books. My first time | Includes index and a list of resources for
    further reading. | Interest age level: 005-008. | Summary: "What
    happens at a funeral or memorial service? These are sometimes held in a
    church or temple so that the person can be remembered for their life.
    While many people at the service will be sad and it may seem scary, one
    way to say good bye at a funeral is to think about the happy times you
    may have had with the person who is gone. Did they make you laugh or
    feel loved? Discover what to expect at a funeral so you will be brave"--
    Provided by publisher.

Identifiers: ISBN 9781643710976 (RLB hardcover) | ISBN 9781643711034
    (softcover) | ISBN 9781643711096 (ebook)

Subjects: LCSH: Funeral rites and ceremonies--Juvenile literature. |
    Grief--Juvenile literature. | Courage--Juvenile literature. | CYAC:
    Funeral rites and ceremonies. | Grief. | Courage.

Classification: LCC GT3150 .C56 2021 (print) | LCC GT3150 (ebook) | DDC
    393/.93--dc23

LCCN: 22020948760

Photo credits: iStock; Shutterstock

Printed in United States of America
0421 1P   CGF21

Table of Contents

What Will Happen?

When someone we love dies, we go to a funeral. A funeral helps us say goodbye.

A funeral can seem scary. We may worry and wonder:

- Will everybody be crying?

- What do I say?

- Will I see the body?

- Do I have to go to the graveyard?

It's normal to worry, but there
is nothing to be afraid of.
Let's look at what happens
when we go to a funeral.

What to Wear

Many people dress up for a funeral. Some people wear all black. Some people may even choose bright colors. Others honor the loved one with important clothes or uniforms to show the dead person's life or interests. Your parents or caregivers can help you decide what to wear.

Good to Know

Black is most often worn to funerals in the US. But people wear white at many Asian funerals. In Korea, you would see people wearing blue.

Spaces and Places

Funerals happen in many places. They can be held in a **funeral home** or a house of worship. Sometimes funeral services are held at the graveside or at another special place. Other times, we remember a loved one in a community space—like a gym or an auditorium.

The Wake

A wake or *visitation* is held the day before the funeral. People wait in line to share good memories or kind words with the family. Sometimes people tell stories and cry. Other times, people tell stories and laugh. Both are good to help people feel better.

Good to Know

People of the Islamic and Jewish faiths usually do not hold wakes. It is important that the dead are buried as quickly as possible.

At a wake you can take your time saying goodbye to the person who died.

History of Wakes

A long time ago, wakes were held in people's homes. Some think it is called a "wake" because family members watched to see if the dead person would wake up! This is probably not true. The word wake meant to watch over or keep **vigil**. The wake was— and still is—a time to grieve the loss of a loved one.

Caskets or Urns

If the person will be buried, the **casket** or **coffin** may be at the wake or funeral. If the casket is open, you can see the body (but you don't have to look!). If it is closed, no one can see the body.

Casket

If the person was **cremated**, an urn may be there. The urn is a container that holds the person's ashes.

Urn

Ashes, bodies, coffins, and urns feel scary! That is normal. You don't have to look at any of them. But seeing them helps some people say goodbye.

The Funeral Service

A funeral service often includes:

- Music

- **Eulogies**

- Prayer and religious **rites**

- Flowers

- Pictures

A funeral director or **clergy** member may lead the service. Friends and family members get up to tell stories as well. Each of these helps us remember and say goodbye to the person who died.

The Burial

If the person will be buried, families and friends form a funeral procession, or long line of cars, and drive to the **cemetery**—or graveyard—or another place of **internment**. There, a few more words are said and the casket is lowered into the ground. Families may throw flowers or toss dirt on top of the casket as a final goodbye.

If the person was cremated, the family may place the urn into a special wall. Or, they might choose another place to spread the ashes.

Saying goodbye may feel sad!

The Meal

After a long day of saying goodbye, it's time to eat together. Families may invite others to their home or a restaurant or back to the house of worship. Over good food, friends and families hug and laugh, tell more stories, and celebrate that life goes on and love never dies.

It can be helpful to remember the life of the dead person with photos and stories.

Words to Know

burial: a ceremony in which a person's body (in a coffin or casket) is lowered into the ground

casket or **coffin:** Both are containers used for burial. A casket is a big rectangle, like a bed with a lid. A coffin is a tapered box to fit a person's body.

cemetery: an place whcrc dead people's bodies or ashes are buried

clergy: a religious leader—like a priest, pastor, rabbi, or imam

cremation: the process of burning a body until it becomes ashes

eulogy: kind words and stories told about a person at a funeral

funeral home: a place where a body is made ready for burial

internment: the process of placing a casket or urn in its final place

rites: ceremonies or procedures held in a service

vigil: a time of staying awake when someone is normally asleep

Learn More at the Library

Check out these books to learn more.

Mundy, Michaelene. *What Happens When Someone Dies? A Child's Guide to Death and Funerals.* Abbey Press. 2014.

Roberts, Dr. Jillian. *What Happens When A Loved One Dies? Our First Talk About Death.* Orca Books, 2016.

Thomas, Pat. *I Miss You: A First Look at Death.* Hodder Childrens Books, 2000.

Index

About the Author

Caryn Rivadeneira writes books for children and serves as Director of Care at her church, which means she goes to or participates in a lot of funerals. When she's not working or writing, Caryn lives with her family and rescued pit bull in the Chicago suburbs.